Managing
Stress

This book was produced in
collaboration with the
**American Institute for
Preventive Medicine.**

1997 printing
Copyright © 1994
New Readers Press
Division of ProLiteracy Worldwide
1320 Jamesville Ave., Syracuse, New York 13210

Information graphics by Shane Kelley
Illustrations by Richard Ewing
Icons by Melanie White
Cover photo: DAVE REVETTE

9 8 7 6 5 4 3 2

Library of Congress Cataloging-in-Publication Data

Managing stress.
p. cm. — (For your information)
"Produced in collaboration with the American
Institute for Preventive Medicine."
ISBN 1-56420-025-6
1. Stress (Psychology) 2. Adjustment (Psychology)
3. Stress management.
I. American Institute for Preventive Medicine.
II. Series: For your information (Syracuse, N.Y.)
BF575.S75M316   1994
155.9'042—dc20   93-40575
                                  CIP

Contents

Preface

Information is power.

Being informed means being able to make choices. When you can make choices, you are not helpless. Having information is the first step toward being in control of a situation. It is a way to get more out of life.

This book, *Managing Stress,* discusses an issue that affects everyone—living with stress. It gives useful information and ideas for controlling the stress in your life.

The books in the For Your Information series are developed with experts from lead agencies in each topic area. This book was developed with help from the American Institute for Preventive Medicine (AIPM). AIPM develops and provides wellness programs and publications. It is based in Farmington Hills, Michigan.

Thanks to the following people for their contribution to the content of *Managing Stress:*

Don R. Powell, Ph.D., founder and president of AIPM; and Elaine Frank, M.Ed., R.D., vice president of AIPM.

And special thanks to Carol J. Moore for her writing.

In this book

- Words in **bold** are explained in the glossary on pages 93–95.

Introduction

You have probably felt **stress** at some time in your life. But what does that mean? And what can you do about it?

The first step is to understand why stress happens. You can feel stress when something bad happens. You can also feel stress when something great happens. Or when nothing special seems to be happening at all.

You've probably learned some ways to deal with normal stress. But sometimes it's hard. You may have new **stressors** in your life. Stressors are things that cause stress. Stress is really the way your body reacts to stressors. You may need new ways to prevent stress or deal with it.

Some people feel worn out and less secure after a high-stress time. They may not know or use good ways to **manage stress.** Other people become stronger each time they get through a high-stress period. They have learned ways to deal with the stress.

The goals of this book are to help you:

- understand what stress is
- identify your own stressors
- learn some ways to manage your stress

This book will show you how to notice stress in your life. There are some self-tests to help you measure your stress. Each chapter suggests ways to manage that stress. Finding ways to deal with stress can improve your life.

How to Use This Book

You can help yourself meet the three goals of this book. One way is to talk over what you read with a friend or family member.

A second way is to keep a **stress notebook.** You don't need to write a lot. Just jot down your ideas. Make lists. Note stressful situations. Note your reactions to them. Draw pictures.

Put the important things you think and do in your notebook. Your thoughts and feelings may

tell you a lot. Reading back over your successes may help you keep going.

A third way to help yourself is to be kind to yourself. Set **short-term goals** such as making an important phone call. Reward yourself for small successes. Expect to make mistakes and keep going if you do.

Small step-by-step changes make a big difference over time. They add up and put you in charge of your life.

Not all the ideas in this book will be right for you. Try some of them. Choose the ones you like and that work for you.

Some Stress Is Good

This book won't teach you how to get rid of stress. Everyone needs some stress just to keep going every day. Some people think all stress is bad. But a moderate level of stress is fine. It is very low or very high levels of stress that cause problems.

Too little stress takes away interest in a task. It's hard to get motivated. Too much stress can be threatening. People under too much stress often worry and feel out of control.

Learning to manage stress is a way of taking control of your life. It is also a way of staying healthy and happy.

Chapter 1

Life Stories

Here are some examples of people who need to reduce their stress. They are not sure how. Imagine they are reading this book, too. At the end, you will see how they have decided to reduce their stress.

Ann

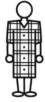 Ann is a newly divorced mother. Her children are 3 and 8 years old. Lately, Ann has had more duties at work. She has little patience with her children. She yells at them often, even for little

things. Ann doesn't listen when the kids have a problem.

Ann knows that she's short-tempered. She took a test once that told her she was a **"Type A" person.** She doesn't like it, but she's not sure how to change. Between the kids and work, she has little time to herself. She used to enjoy spending time with her friends. Now she doesn't even feel like calling them.

Ann is very tired by the end of the day, but she has trouble sleeping. She takes two hours to get to sleep. Then she tosses and turns all night.

Robert

Robert is a 22-year-old machine operator. He just started his new job. He feels he doesn't fit in well. Robert lives with his father, who is an alcoholic. He puts Robert down all the time, and tells him that he's a failure.

At work, Robert just does his job and doesn't say much. Sometimes he disagrees with his boss about doing something. But he just does it the way his boss wants. Then he's angry at himself for not saying anything.

Neither Robert nor his father likes to cook. Most nights, they order pizza, or microwave something. Other times, they don't eat at all, or

Robert has a bowl of cereal for dinner. Sometimes, he gets drunk with his father because there's nothing else to do.

Jon

 Jon is a 52-year-old salesclerk. His wife just died of a heart attack. Jon can't stop thinking about her. Every day, he misses her. He worries about dying. He can't get the thought of it out of his mind.

Since his wife died, Jon has been working a lot of overtime. He thinks this will keep his mind off her death.

Jon smokes a lot more than before. He even smokes instead of eating.

He has let the apartment get in a real mess. He feels that there is no one to keep it clean for. He leaves dishes in the sink for days. He doesn't empty the ashtrays.

Jon's sister stopped by one Sunday. She couldn't believe the mess. She asked him what was going on. He seemed under stress. She suggested he ask his doctor for help in dealing with the stress.

Chapter 2

What Is Stress?

Many different things cause stress. Some are everyday things. Others are major changes in your life. A few examples are listed below:

- noise
- traffic
- long lines
- constant change and new demands
- death of a loved one
- sickness or injury
- losing a job

- poor lighting
- crowded work space
- being too hot or too cold
- cigarettes, alcohol, or other drugs
- too much **caffeine**
- winning the lottery
- graduating
- getting married
- divorce
- problems in relationships
- having too much to do every day
- arguments
- a difficult boss
- having a baby
- failing a test
- a huge bill
- your car breaking down

These events are stressors. Your body's response to these demands is stress.

Events That Cause Stress

It is easy to see that real events can cause stress. Worrying about events can also cause stress, even if the events never happen.

Many people think that stress results only from bad events. That is not true. A happy event like getting married can also cause stress.

People choose or plan some stressors such as taking the GED, retirement, or getting married. These stressors are likely to cause less stress than unwanted, unplanned, and unhappy stressors.

How you see things can also cause stress. Thinking that something is bad can make it bad. The same event that creates a lot of stress for some people may just annoy others.

For example, some people get angry when they are cut off in traffic. Others hardly notice. Some people are more stressed by having a cavity filled than by a traffic ticket. Others are more stressed by the ticket.

Coping with Stress

Your body reacts to stress. For example, suppose someone jumped out at you in the dark. It could be a mugger. Or it could be a friend playing a joke.

In either case, your body reacts with alarm. Your heart beats faster. You start to sweat. You have more energy. Afterward, you feel exhausted.

Not all stressors cause the same kind of fear as being mugged. But all stressors place some demand on the body.

Some people worry about everything, large or small. This takes a lot of energy. If you worry a lot, you may develop health problems.

You need to face what's worrying you. If you can do something about it, take action. If you can't do anything about it, try to change your outlook. If you take care of yourself and keep going, this is called **coping.**

You can learn coping skills. This book will give you lots of coping ideas. You can choose the ones that work best for you. Coping with stress is also called managing stress.

People manage stress in different ways. Some people walk or run. Some people shop. Some sleep. Others watch TV.

Stressors can become too big for normal ways of coping, however. That can happen when there is any major change in a person's life.

Sometimes a series of smaller stressors happen over a short period of time. Perhaps you argue with someone you care about. Then you get a big bill. Then your baby gets sick. The stressors add up.

When stressors become too great, your **stress level** keeps going up. Your body works harder and harder to stay well and fight sickness. If too much stress continues for a long time, you may become ill.

The next chapter can help you find your stress level. Then you can work on managing your stress if you need to.

Chapter 3

Finding Your Stress Level

This chapter includes four self-tests to measure your stress level. These self-tests will give you a general sense of the stress in your life. Use all of them, or use the one that is best for you.

- **Life events scale.** Take this self-test if your life has changed a lot lately.

- **Signs of stress.** Take this self-test if you've had a lot of health problems lately.

- **Type A behavior.** Take this self-test if little things cause you to feel stress.
- **Burnout.** Try this checklist if you feel you are not working as well as you should be.

Life Events Scale

You know that some events in your life cause stress. But do you know how much stress different events cause? You can measure this using the self-test on page 21.

The test was developed by Dr. Thomas Holmes and Dr. Richard Rahe. They noticed that patients with high stress were likely to get sick. So they measured the link between stress and illness.

Their scale gives a number value to 43 life events. The scale helps you see that stress is a normal response to life events. Being stressed is not a personal weakness.

The scale also shows you your own stress level. If it shows that you are in a high-stress period, you need to find ways to cope.

What is your stress level on the life events scale? To find out, check off the events that have happened to you in the past year. If something happened more than once, place a check for each time it took place. Then add up the units for those events.

Life event	Units	Checks	Your score
death of a spouse	100	_____	_____
divorce	73	_____	_____
separating from a spouse	65	_____	_____
serving time in jail	63	_____	_____
death of a close family member	63	_____	_____
own injury or illness	53	_____	_____
getting married	50	_____	_____
being fired	47	_____	_____
getting back together with a spouse	45	_____	_____
retirement	45	_____	_____
change in family member's health	44	_____	_____
pregnancy of self or spouse	40	_____	_____
sex problems	39	_____	_____
adding a family member	39	_____	_____
change within a job	39	_____	_____
change in finances	38	_____	_____
death of a close friend	37	_____	_____
changing to a new line of work	36	_____	_____
change in number of arguments with your spouse	35	_____	_____
debt over $10,000	31	_____	_____
foreclosure of a loan	30	_____	_____
change in job duties	29	_____	_____
child leaving home	29	_____	_____
trouble with in-laws	29	_____	_____
outstanding personal victory	28	_____	_____
spouse began or stopped work	26	_____	_____

(continued)

start or end of school	26	_____	_____
change in living conditions	25	_____	_____
change in personal habits	24	_____	_____
trouble with your boss	23	_____	_____
change in work hours	20	_____	_____
moving to another home	20	_____	_____
changing schools	20	_____	_____
changing leisure activities	19	_____	_____
changing church activities	19	_____	_____
changing social activities	18	_____	_____
debt of less than $10,000	17	_____	_____
changing sleep patterns	16	_____	_____
change in number of family get-togethers	15	_____	_____
changing eating habits	15	_____	_____
vacation	13	_____	_____
major holiday	12	_____	_____
minor problem with the law	11	_____	_____
Your total units			_____

How to rate your stress:

- 150–199 or lower: You are pretty safe.
- 200–299: You have had moderately high stress. You may want to learn some new ways to manage stress.
- 300 or higher: You have had a high degree of stress. Your chances of becoming ill are greater. That doesn't mean you have to become sick. Instead, you need to find ways to cope with stress.

Signs of Stress

You may not score high on the life events scale but still feel a lot of stress. In this case, you may need to look for other signs of stress.

Signs of too much stress vary from person to person. Notice any stress signals that your body is sending. Look at the list of signals below. Check off any that you have.

Behavioral signs of stress

_____	accident-prone
_____	clearing throat often
_____	clenching hands
_____	crying a lot
_____	driving recklessly
_____	using drugs
_____	drumming fingers
_____	forgetting things a lot
_____	grinding teeth
_____	nervous laughing
_____	overeating
_____	sexual problems
_____	sleep problems
_____	smoking or drinking more
_____	stuttering
_____	tapping foot

Physical signs of stress

_____ acne

_____ backache

_____ hard bowel movements

_____ diarrhea

_____ dizziness

_____ eyestrain

_____ headaches

_____ heart pounding

_____ high blood pressure

_____ missed periods

_____ muscle tension

_____ neck pains

_____ nervous tics

_____ skin rashes

_____ sleep changes

_____ stomach pains

_____ sweating often

_____ dry throat and mouth

_____ tension

_____ tiredness

_____ trembling

_____ ulcers

_____ urinating often

_____ weakness

_____ weight changes

Emotional signs of stress

_____ anxious

_____ depressed

_____ hyperactive

_____ impulsive

_____ irritated often

_____ mood swings

_____ racing thoughts

_____ wandering thoughts

If you checked any of these items, your body may be sending stress signals. You need to find some new ways to manage your stress. Otherwise, you may get sick.

Type A Behavior

You can predict many stressors. Traffic is going to be heavy right after work. There will be a long line at the bank on payday.

People react to long lines and delays in different ways. Some get upset. Their stomachs get upset. They may be restless and complain. They use up a lot of energy. But they cannot change the situation.

Others remain calm. They watch what is going on. They let their thoughts wander to something more pleasant. Perhaps they listen to the radio or a tape.

What is the difference between these behaviors? Some people are restless and nervous. They may be easily irritated or quick to anger. They don't trust other people. They are said to have Type A behavior.

Some people are low-key. They do things one at a time. They speak slowly. People who are calm are said to have **"Type B" behavior.**

Some people with Type A behavior are much more likely to suffer from heart disease than Type Bs.

Type A people often expect too much of themselves. They want to be perfect. They expect to get a lot done. They feel time pressure even when they work hard and fast.

Do you have Type A behavior? Take the self-test on page 27 to find out. If you checked Yes to more than six questions, you tend toward Type A behavior. You may want to look for some new ways to become more like a Type B.

Burnout

One sign of too much stress is **burnout.** That is when problems become so overpowering, they prevent you from living a normal life.

 **Self-Test**

Do you have Type A ways?

Check under Yes or No for each question.

	Yes	No
Do you get impatient easily?	___	___
Do you try to do two or more things at a time?	___	___
Do you usually have more to do than time to do it in?	___	___
Do other people think you're intense?	___	___
Do you interrupt people when they are talking to you?	___	___
Do you always compare yourself to others?	___	___
Do you find it hard to say no?	___	___
Do you have habits like grinding your teeth or drumming your fingers?	___	___
Do you speak critically about others?	___	___
Do you feel guilty if you relax or take time off?	___	___

 **Self-Test**

Are you burnt out?

Check under Yes or No for each question.

	Yes	No
Do you get tired more easily now?	___	___
Have people been saying, "You don't look so good"?	___	___
Do you work harder but get less done?	___	___
Do you feel sad for no reason?	___	___
Do you forget things more often?	___	___
Are you more short-tempered?	___	___
Do you spend less time with friends?	___	___
Do you feel too busy for even routine tasks?	___	___
Do you have more aches and pains?	___	___
Does sex seem like more trouble than it's worth?	___	___
Do you have little to say to people?	___	___

Are you burnt out? Take the self-test on page 28 to find out. Think back to six months ago. How did you feel then? Compare that with how you feel now. If you checked Yes to five or more of these questions, you may be heading for burnout. If you checked Yes to more than eight of them, you need some new ways to cope.

The next chapters can help you learn to cope with stress.

Chapter 4

Relaxing

Living in these times can be stressful. To stay healthy, people need to relax. Relaxing helps reduce stress.

Relaxing is a skill. It means more than getting away from your daily routine. It means "turning off" your mind for a while. Relaxing should make you feel peaceful and calm. It should help you think more clearly. Relaxing can also reduce pain.

One way to relax is to do something you enjoy. Look at the list of quick ways to relax on page 31. Check under "Do now" for any that you do. Check under "Try" for any you would like to try. And add a few ideas of your own.

Quick ways to relax

	Do now	Try
take a walk or exercise	_____	_____
do some outdoor chores	_____	_____
play with a child or pet	_____	_____
take a warm bath or shower	_____	_____
plan an imaginary trip	_____	_____
play music you enjoy	_____	_____
sit still and look around you	_____	_____
watch a funny movie	_____	_____
wear comfortable clothes	_____	_____
drink herbal tea	_____	_____
call a friend	_____	_____
take a picnic to a park	_____	_____
watch the sun set	_____	_____
repair or clean something	_____	_____
take a nap	_____	_____
play a game or do a puzzle	_____	_____

You can also practice exercises that relax your mind and body. Some are included in this chapter. Try the ones that fit your lifestyle or that you enjoy.

Learning to relax takes practice. You need to train both your body and your mind. Whatever exercises you choose, do them at least once a day. Twice is better.

Deep breathing

You might think that breathing happens naturally. That is true. But we don't breathe as deeply as we can. People sit with poor posture. They wear tight clothes. They smoke. They breathe harmful chemicals.

Every time you are tense, your breathing changes. Usually, the more stress you feel, the more **shallow** your breathing becomes. Then your body does not get the oxygen it needs. You may feel sleepy or edgy. You may get a headache.

Deep breathing can help you relax. It also helps lower your heart rate and **blood pressure.**

You can't fully expand your lungs with every breath. But it is good to do so some of the time. Try this exercise:

- Sit in a chair. Set your feet apart and get comfortable. Put your arms at your sides.
- Slowly draw your breath in through your nose. Take a long, steady breath. Allow your chest to fill with air.
- Hold the air for three seconds.
- Let your breath out slowly through your mouth. Make a relaxing "whooshing" sound.
- Keep inhaling long, slow, deep breaths and letting them out in the same way. Listen to the sound of the deep breathing. Think about how it feels.
- Continue for three to five minutes.

Letting your mind wander

Set aside about 15 minutes a day to clear your mind and let your thoughts wander. You may find this very calming.

- Find a quiet place as far away from noise as possible. Sit or lie in a comfortable position. Try to relax your body.
- Close your eyes. Let your mind wander. Try not to think of anything. Hum if you feel like it.
- Open your eyes slowly when you're ready. You'll probably feel relaxed and refreshed.

Relaxing your muscles

Tension builds up in your muscles. You can relax them with this exercise:

- Lie flat on the floor, a bed, or a couch. Find a comfortable position and close your eyes. Take a few slow, deep breaths.
- Tighten all the muscles around your eyes and forehead. Hold them tight, then relax them. As you release the muscles, imagine your stress floating away.
- Continue to repeat this tightening and letting go for each muscle group in your body. Move to these muscles: mouth, jaw,

neck, shoulders, back, arms, hands, buttocks, upper legs, lower legs, feet.

Always start at your head and work your way down to your toes. Each time you relax a set of muscles, picture the stress leaving your body.

- Stay lying down for a few minutes after you are done. Get up slowly and enjoy the relaxed feeling.

Another way to relax some muscles is to hold a pen in your hand. Tighten your hand around the pen. Hold it tight for about 30 seconds. Then release the pen. Repeat the exercise a couple of times.

Creating a mental picture

The mind affects the body. Sometimes, it's hard to make your mind tell your body to relax. Picturing a relaxing place can give both your mind and your body a break.

- Sit back in a chair and get as comfortable as you can. Gently close your eyes. Relax your muscles.
- Take a few slow, deep breaths. Hold them and let them out slowly.
- Picture yourself in any place you want to be—perhaps the beach, the woods, or the

mountains. Enjoy the sights, sounds, smells, and feel of the place.
- Think about this special place for 15 minutes. Just relax and be there. Imagine the sunset and the night coming.
- As you feel ready, slowly open your eyes. You will probably feel totally refreshed.

Stretching and yawning

Sometimes a yawn is very relaxing. So is a good, long body stretch. Stand or lie down and stretch every part of you, like a cat does. Shake any areas that still feel tight. Move slowly. Enjoy the way stretching feels. This is easy to do and takes very little time.

Chapter 5

Taking Control of Your Time

Everyone has the same 24 hours in a day. But some people get more out of those hours than others. They are people who manage their time well.

Other people may rush. They put things off. They miss deadlines. They don't take care of their own needs. This all adds to their stress.

No one has total control over their daily life. Someone or something always makes demands. But you have some control—and probably more than you think.

This chapter will help you improve your use of time. It will show you how to:

- set goals and **priorities**
- cut down on time wasters
- learn not to put things off
- increase your useful time by planning

The first step is knowing how you spend your time now. Look at the list of activities on page 39. Write down about how much time you spend on each of them in a normal day. Add other things that you do.

If you can't remember how much time you spend on different things, you could keep a **time log.** For a week, write down everything you do and how long it takes.

Look over how you are spending your time. Do you think you're wasting some of it? How can you spend more of it doing what you want to do? Setting goals can help.

Setting Goals and Priorities

Setting goals and priorities takes a lot of time and thought. But it helps give you more control over your time and your life. That helps reduce stress and make your daily life more enjoyable.

Where does the time go?

Activity	How much time?
grooming (dressing, showering, etc.)	————————
eating	————————
sleeping	————————
exercising	————————
being with friends	————————
getting to work	————————
working or looking for work	————————
caring for children	————————
shopping	————————
doing housework or other chores	————————
paying bills	————————
working on hobbies	————————
watching TV	————————
listening to music	————————
reading	————————

What is important to you? What do you want to be doing with your life now? What do you want to be doing in five years? Use this method to start working toward some **long-term goals.**

1. Get a piece of paper. Write these headings on it:
   Personal
   Work
   Family
   Education
   Fun
   Leave some space for writing between each heading.

2. Think about your goals. Jot down as many goals as you can under each heading. Put down whatever comes to mind, even if it seems silly.

3. Go back and label your goals "long-term" and "short-term." An example of a long-term goal would be getting a better job. A short-term goal might be cleaning your kitchen.

4. Choose the long-term goals that are most important to you. Write each goal down on a separate piece of paper. List the steps you must take to reach each goal.

5. Now look at the steps. Be realistic. Are you willing to spend time doing them?

Can you do them? If you answer no to several steps, cross out the goal. It may not be that important to you. You now have a group of long-term goals and steps to reach them.

6. Decide which short-term goals are most important. Set deadlines for doing each one. Start working toward them as soon as you can.

Time Wasters

One way to use time wisely is to cut down on time wasters. Time wasters may be tasks that don't really need to be done. Time wasters come from not being organized, never saying no, and putting things off. They come from people who interrupt you or who are always late. Spending free time with people who don't help you relax is another time waster.

Here are some tips to help you cut down on time wasters:

1. Learn to say no to tasks and people who do not help you meet your goals.

2. Nobody can do everything perfectly. Decide which things need to be done with care. Be less careful with the rest.

3. Set aside time when you don't let anyone interrupt you, not even a phone call. When someone interrupts you, stand up. This will help keep the talk short.

4. Keep things in their place. Don't waste time looking for keys, tools, and utensils.

5. Make use of waiting time. Carry a notebook and jot down things you need to do. Read a magazine.

Learning Not to Put Things Off

Do you put things off? It may be why you're not getting enough done.

Some people put things off on purpose. Others put things off but don't know they are doing it. They:

- can't make a decision
- feel tired when they think of the task
- are waiting until "things slow down"
- have already missed a deadline, so think "What's the difference?"

Here are some tips to help you stop putting things off:

- Commit. Promise somebody else that you'll complete the task. Someone else will be counting on you. You'll be more likely to follow through.
- Ask. Get more information. Ask for more detail. If you are unclear about a task, you will not feel ready to start it.
- Break up tasks. Think of large tasks as a group of smaller tasks. Keep a list of the small tasks and do them when you have small amounts of time.
- Use time that you didn't expect to have. Canceled dates are a chance to catch up.

Use the time to do a task you have been avoiding.

- Use your energy. Start hard tasks when your energy is highest. Some people do better in the morning; others do best later in the day. Make use of your best times.
- Remember goals. Remind yourself of your goals. Ask yourself why you are doing a task. Think about the benefits of finishing it. Think of what will happen if it doesn't get done.
- Reward. Pat yourself on the back. When you finish a task, treat yourself to a break or some other reward.
- Do it. The best way to begin is to begin.

Planning

Planning helps you increase your useful time. It tells you how to get from where you are to where you want to be. A plan lists the things you need to get there. It tells you when to begin each step and how long it should take.

Here are some tips for planning:

- Long-term plans list what you expect to get done over a period of months. You need to break them down into weekly plans.

- Plan large blocks of time for tasks that need it. Use an up-to-date **master calendar.**

- Learn how much time you need. Write down how long you expect a task to take. Then keep track of the actual time spent. Compare them. This will help you allow enough time in your future plans.

- Make a "to do" list every morning. Keep it handy. Only include the things you really plan to do that day. Check off the things that you get done. Make one list for work and one for home.

- Rate your tasks:
  A—must do
  B—should do
  C—would like to do

  Write A next to items on your "to do" list that you *must* do. Put B next to those you *should* do. And put C beside the less important items. Spend time on the As. Get help with some of the Bs and Cs.

  Notice that a B or C may become an A as a deadline approaches. An A can become a C if things change.

- Don't promise to do too much. Leave some room for unexpected things.

- Balance quiet work and activity in your plans.

Chapter 6

Listening and Speaking Skills

You spend a lot of time talking to people and listening to them. So you must be pretty good at it, right?

Not so, if you are like most people. Too often, people spend their listening time planning what they will say next. Or they jump on the first few words and think they know the rest.

When people don't listen well, they often don't understand. They don't find out what the other person wants, needs, or thinks. Such misunderstanding often leads to stress.

Listening Skills

How do you become a good listener? First, try not to put up blocks to good listening. Blocks include actions like these:

- comparing yourself to the speaker
- trying to read the speaker's mind
- listening to only part of the message
- letting your mind wander
- giving advice the speaker is not asking for
- arguing with the speaker
- judging or being critical
- interrupting

- twisting the facts in order to be right
- changing the topic before the speaker is done
- pretending to agree when you don't

Good listeners avoid these blocks. They also practice skills that make them better listeners.

Good listeners look at you, smile, and nod their heads. They ask questions and rephrase what they hear. They really want to understand you correctly. They pay attention to both words and body signals. They notice if your fist is clenched or if you have tears in your eyes.

Active listening

Good listeners are active listeners. The goal of active listening is to let other people know that you do hear how they think and feel.

Active listening involves saying back in your own words what the person is saying or feeling. ("You seem to be angry at your mother.")

It also means making sure you understand, or asking for more information. ("Is this what you mean?")

Feedback is part of active listening, too. It means sharing some thoughts on what you heard.

Practice all these methods. You can also follow these tips for building listening skills:

- Decide that you want to understand the other person's point of view.
- Stand or sit close to the speaker.
- Look for the speaker's main ideas.
- Look for ideas or feelings you have in common.
- Keep an open mind.
- Make understanding your goal, not agreement.
- Plan to tell the information to someone else.

Speaking Up for Yourself

Good listening will reduce stress in your dealings with others. But you also have to express your own needs. You can talk about your needs without harming others.

Family members, friends, and co-workers all need to know what your needs and goals are. You can probably talk more easily with some of these people than with others.

How easily do you assert yourself? Read the list below. Put a 1 after activities that make you feel a little uncomfortable. Put a 2 by those that make you feel very uncomfortable.

	1 or 2
returning an item to a store	_____
making a business appointment	_____
asking for a favor	_____
speaking in public	_____
complaining about poor service	_____
getting a review from the boss	_____
disagreeing with a friend	_____
asking a stranger for directions	_____
being critical of a friend	_____
questioning someone's decision	_____

telling someone you are angry _____

speaking up when you are cheated _____

saying no to an invitation _____

saying no to a pushy salesperson _____

shushing someone at a movie _____

asking for a date _____

asking for a loan _____

expressing an opinion
   that differs from the group's _____

Total _____

Add up your score.

1–7: You are assertive.

8–16: You could practice to become more assertive.

16–30: You are uncomfortable with being assertive. This may be causing you stress.

There are many benefits to expressing your needs clearly and directly. They include:

- being able to ask for help
- being more clearly understood
- saying no without feeling guilty
- being more responsible for yourself
- finding that others listen to you
- doing more of what you like to do

Practicing being direct

The **LADDER** is a tool to help you learn and practice skills in being direct with people. It will help you express your needs tactfully.

Step 1: Look at your needs, wants, rights, and feelings. (I'm too tired. My daughter has been playing loud music very late every night.)

Decide what you want to do. (I will tell her she can't play her music after 11 o'clock.)

Step 2: Arrange a meeting with the person you need to talk to. Pick a time that is good for both of you and a place that is relaxed.

Step 3: Define the problem. Be clear about it. (I'm not getting enough sleep.)

Step 4: Describe your feelings using **"I-messages."** I-messages do not blame the other person for how you feel. This is true even if the other person's behavior is the problem. (Say "I feel anxious because I can't do well when I am so tired." Avoid saying "You shouldn't play your music so loud.")

Step 5: Express a plan for solving the problem. Look the person in the eye. Stand or sit tall. Use a clear, calm voice. ("I'd like you to stop playing music by 11 o'clock at night.")

Step 6: Reward the other person for changing their behavior. Tell them what the benefits will be. ("You can play your music loud on

Saturday afternoons.") Reward yourself for your own efforts.

At first it may not be easy to express your needs directly. To express yourself well you need to:

- Care about yourself.
- Know your strengths and abilities.
- Know your rights. Stand up for yourself.
- Look at your needs. Figure out a way to meet them.
- Tell others about your needs clearly and without blame.
- Believe that your needs are as important as anyone else's.
- Say no without feeling guilty.

Chapter 7

Exercising

Movement is a sign of life. Active movement (exercise) helps reduce tension in your body. Tension may be causing headaches, backaches, and general discomfort. Exercise increases the power of your heart and lungs. It makes your body strong and increases your energy.

Jobs often involve sitting for many hours or standing in an assembly line. We don't move as much as people once did. Now we need to exercise our bodies to be healthy.

Active movement also releases chemicals that calm you down and help reduce stress.

When you are nervous or angry, do something active. Run, walk, scrub the floor. You will get rid of your "uptight" feeling.

Activity also helps keep your body fit. It gives you energy and confidence. It makes you able to do more.

Some people hate the idea of exercise. But it can be fun. The key is to choose something that suits you and that you enjoy. That way, you're more likely to stick with it.

The self-test on page 56 can help you find out what exercise is best for you. If you start an exercise program, it is important to do something that is fun. Do it with a friend if you don't like doing things by yourself. Do it alone if you prefer quiet time.

Aerobic Exercise

Some people choose to do **aerobic exercise** one day, then take a slow walk or do something easy the next day. It is a good idea to vary your activities so that you use different muscles.

There are many ways to get aerobic exercise. They include jogging, running, swimming, dancing, hiking, biking, skipping rope, and playing basketball or tennis.

The word *aerobics* means exercise that is active enough to increase your heart and

✓ Self-Test

What exercise is for you?

Choose one answer to each question and
write it on the blank.

Do you like to be indoors or outdoors?   _____

Do you like to be alone or with others?   _____

Do you like to compete or
go at your own pace?   _____

Can you afford to take classes or
join a health club?   _____

What activities fit your body type?   _____

What activities do you enjoy?   _____

breathing rates. It's been proved that aerobic exercise reduces stress. Fit people can deal better with the demands of their lives. Aerobic exercise works this way because it:

- improves health
- increases the flow of blood and oxygen to all parts of your body
- strengthens your heart, reducing the chances of a heart attack
- increases your energy

- decreases fat and increases lean muscle
- leads to a firmer, stronger body
- allows more restful sleep
- decreases nervous energy and depression
- releases muscle tension
- improves how you feel about yourself

It is a good idea to talk with a doctor before starting an exercise program. This is even more important if:

- you are over 40 and haven't been exercising regularly

- you have a medical problem
- you haven't had a checkup in a while

Aerobic exercise guidelines

If you are going to start an exercise program, follow these guidelines:

- Begin slowly. Start with 5–10 minutes of active exercise and slowly increase it.
- Always start with some stretches. They prepare your body for activity and help prevent injury. End exercise the same way.
- Breathe in as your movements expand. You should be able to talk as you exercise.
- Normal breathing should return in 10 minutes after exercising. If it doesn't, you are exercising too hard.
- Watch for your body's warning signs. If pain starts, or if you feel faint or dizzy, stop right away.
- Exercise at least three times a week. Work up to 20 minutes or longer each time.
- Plan your activity ahead of time. Mark it on a calendar.
- Choose types of exercise you will enjoy. Vary what you do. The goal is to have fun and stay interested.

Exercise in Your Daily Life

There are also many small ways to build exercise into your daily tasks.

At home, walk around as much as you can. Get up to change TV stations. Stretch while brushing your teeth or drying your hair. Wash the car or mow a lawn briskly.

When you are out, try to use stairs rather than the elevator. Get off the bus or park your car a block or two from where you're going and walk. Walk briskly when shopping at a mall.

Sitting exercises

Many of us sit for long periods of time. Did you know that you can help tone your muscles and reduce stress without leaving your chair? Here are some ways to make your sitting more active. Do these exercises two or three times a day.

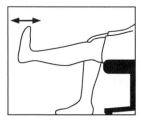

Leg stretches. Lift one leg in front of you. Point and flex your toes. Lower your leg. Repeat five times with each leg.

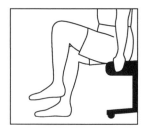

Knee lifts. Sit near the front edge of your chair. Hold on to the side of the chair. Lift first one knee, then the other, for about a minute.

Neck/shoulder stretch. Place your right hand against the left side of your head, above the ear. Pull your head to the right while you push against it to the left. To increase the stretch, reach your left arm toward the floor. Do the same with your left hand. Repeat five times on each side.

Head circles. Drop your head to the left, then bring it back to the center. Drop it to the right, then bring it back to the center. Drop it to the front, then bring it back to the center. Drop it to the back, then bring it back to the center. Repeat five times.

Shoulder to ear. Lift both shoulders as if you were trying to touch your ears. Hold. Relax and repeat five times.

Arm reaches. Lift your arms overhead one at a time. Pretend you're trying to reach the ceiling. Repeat five times with each arm.

Sleep

Exercise helps you sleep well. Your body needs sleep to stay well and to reduce stress. Lack of sleep can lead to stress. And stress itself can upset sleeping patterns.

Different people need different amounts of sleep. But most people need from six to eight hours a day.

If you wake up often or have nightmares, you aren't getting the right kind of sleep. The methods in this book can help you get deep, full sleep.

If you have problems with your sleeping, try some of these tips:

- Don't eat or drink for two hours before going to bed.
- Go to bed when you are ready. Don't try to sleep when you feel awake.
- Try to think of bedtime as a positive way to end the day.

- Keep your bedroom at a comfortable temperature.
- Do something relaxing before trying to sleep. Take a warm bath, listen to music, or talk quietly.
- Follow good nutrition and exercise guidelines.

Stress in your mind can cause problems with your body. But taking care of your body can sometimes help to relieve stress in your mind.

Chapter 8

Eating Healthy Food

What people eat has a lot to do with how they feel. The right food is important to well-being. The wrong food increases stress in people's bodies.

It is easy to be confused about which foods and drinks to buy. Ads can tempt you with sweet treats and quick fixes. The food do's and don'ts keep changing.

Food companies may label foods with words like "lo" and "lite." But the food still may not be good for you.

There is no single food plan that everyone should follow. But there are helpful guidelines.

You can use them to develop eating habits that are good for you.

In general, good diets are low in fat and high in **fiber**. They include plenty of fruits, vegetables, and whole grains. They also include small amounts of **protein,** such as meat, chicken, turkey, fish, dairy products (eggs, cheese, milk, etc.), and beans.

Some elements in foods increase the stress on our bodies. They include:

- **Caffeine.** Caffeine can increase your heart rate, blood pressure, and feelings of **anxiety.** Your body may act as if it is under stress.

- **Sugar.** It can cause highs and lows in your blood sugar levels. It can cause mood

changes and headaches. Sugar keeps some people from sleeping well. It may make children **hyperactive.**

- **Salt.** It makes your body retain water. It can lead to high blood pressure. High blood pressure often leads to heart disease.

If you eat a good diet, your body gets the vitamins it needs. B vitamins help keep stress under control. You may want to take B vitamin supplements as well as eat a good diet.

Track Your Eating Habits

Many times people turn to food because they are bored or angry, not hungry. And they may eat **"junk food"** such as candy, cookies, or potato chips.

Junk food deprives the body of needed vitamins and minerals. People may feel guilty about eating junk food. But habits are hard to break.

How can you begin to use food to help you handle stress? First, take an honest look at what you eat. Also, try to understand why you eat.

You need to listen to what your body is telling you about food. Then you can make clearer choices about food and its part in your life.

- Keep a **food log** for two weeks. Write down what you eat and how much. Also write down where you ate it and who you were with.

- Notice how hungry your body feels. Think of a scale of 1 (fainting with hunger) to 10 (overstuffed). Before you eat anything, ask yourself where your hunger fits on this scale. Try not to eat unless your hunger is at level five or lower.

- Learn the difference between stomach hunger and mouth hunger. Mouth hunger is when you want to chew on or taste something but your body doesn't need food. Try gum or mints to satisfy mouth hunger.

- Notice your body's signals. Is your tongue discolored or does it feel coated? Do you have bad breath or a sour taste in your mouth? Do your teeth get cavities? Are your fingernails split? Do you get headaches a lot? These can be signs that you need to change your diet. Check with a doctor if you want help.

- Notice how you feel after eating a meal. If you feel heavy or too full, you may be eating too much.

- Notice how you sleep. If you have trouble
  sleeping, think what food and drink you
  had in the evening. Heavy foods, sweets,
  caffeine, or alcohol can make it hard to
  sleep.
- Try different foods and ways of eating.
  Add a food or take away a food for a
  while. Try eating your main meal earlier in
  the day. Try not to snack during the
  evening. Let enough time go by to see if
  changes are helpful to you.

Guidelines for Healthy Eating

1. Eat three meals a day.

2. Drink plenty of water between meals. (See page 71.)

3. Eat a variety of food every day. This provides the **nutrients** your body needs to be healthy. Nutrients are the materials your body gets from food. Choose from:
   - fresh fruits
   - fresh vegetables
   - whole-grain, enriched breads and cereals
   - skim milk, low-fat cheese, and low-fat yogurt
   - meats, chicken, and fish
   - nuts and dried peas and beans

4. Cut down on the number of processed foods you eat. They often have too much salt and sugar, and too many **additives.**

5. Limit your sugar intake.
   - Eat less candy, cakes, and cookies.
   - Select canned fruits without sugar added.
   - Don't drink sodas that contain sugar.

- When baking, increase the amount of vanilla and spices, and reduce the sugar.
- Read labels. Words like sucrose, glucose, maltose, dextrose, lactose, fructose, and syrups all mean that sugar is present.

6. Cut down on fats and **cholesterol.** They are linked with heart disease. A high-fat diet is linked to cancer. To cut down:

- Limit animal fats.
- Limit red meats. Use lean cuts. Trim fat.
- Choose fish, skinless chicken, and dried beans and peas for protein.
- Bake, broil, or steam rather than fry.
- Limit eggs.
- Use skim or low-fat milk.
- Limit butter, cream, and shortening. Use small amounts of liquid vegetable oils or soft margarines.

7. Limit salt.

- Take the salt shaker off the table.
- Cook with herbs and spices instead.
- Limit these foods that are often high in salt: canned and frozen foods, prepared meats like ham and lunch meats, salted snack foods.
- Read labels. If sodium is listed, the food contains the harmful part of salt.

8. Reduce caffeine. Keep it to less than 250 milligrams (mg) a day. Better yet, try to stop using caffeine. It is found in:

- regular coffee (about 192 mg per 8-ounce cup)
- instant coffee (about 96 mg per 8-ounce cup)
- tea (about 56 mg per 8-ounce cup)
- sodas and colas (about 50 mg per 12 ounces)
- chocolate (about 20 mg per ounce)

Drink plenty of water

Eating healthy food is important. So is drinking plenty of water.

Water makes up about 70 percent of your body's weight. Your body needs water for

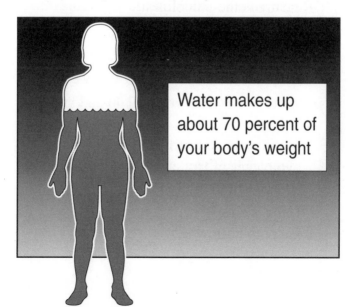

Water makes up about 70 percent of your body's weight

cooling, digesting food, and sending food to every cell. It needs water for flushing out toxins (poisonous substances) from food and air.

Too little water can cause headaches, pain, and stiffness. It can make bowel movements hard.

For good health and energy, drink six to eight big glasses of water a day. Don't think that other liquids will do the trick. They often contain caffeine or sugar, which use up body fluids.

Getting Started

Sometimes it is hard to know what to do with all this advice about diet. Where do you start? Changing your diet to manage stress should not cause you stress.

Here are some guidelines:

- Don't try to change too much at once.
- Choose one or two of the guidelines. Plan to follow them for the next few weeks.
- Write down what you will do and how long you will do it. For example, you could write, "For three weeks I will eat two pieces of fruit a day and I will stop adding salt to my food."
- Hang the paper with your plan in the kitchen. Follow it.

- When the time is up, add another step. "Now for three weeks I will also eat one serving of raw or fresh cooked vegetables a day."
- Keep making changes slowly and one step at a time.

Chapter 9

New Thinking Patterns

We often face events that cause stress. The way we think about the events may add to or reduce our stress. Changing your **thinking patterns** can lower your stress.

Distorted Thinking

Do you feel like your stress is caused by other people or by events outside your control? This may be **distorted thinking.** People increase their stress with distorted thinking. Such thinking comes from looking at only one part of a situation.

The chart on page 77 lists some kinds of distorted thinking. You can use the chart to find out if the way you think adds to your stress. As you read each question, ask yourself if you ever think that way. Think of examples from your life. This can show you what kinds of distorted thinking you may be doing. They are the ones you need to pay attention to.

Changing thinking patterns

Here are some tips you can use to fight distorted thinking:

- Stop saying that things are terrible or awful. Don't use the phrase "I can't stand it." You probably can stand it.
- Avoid **absolutes.** Use words like "may" and "sometimes." Don't say absolute things like "No one will ever love me."
- Think in percentages. People are not all good or all bad, totally smart or totally stupid. Think, "This goes wrong about 60 percent of the time."
- Find proof. How much proof do you have for your decisions? Does it come from just one or two cases? Can you make different decisions from the same proof?

- Be specific. Limit what you think to a specific case. Do not try to make it fit every other case.
- Check it out. Treat your ideas about people as guesses. Check them out by asking if they are true.
- Rethink your "shoulds." Think of exceptions to all your "rules." Know that what works for you may not work for someone else.
- Don't be labeled by a feeling. You may feel foolish in a situation. But that doesn't make you a fool. You are not what you feel.

Distorted Thinking

Do you . . .	If you do, you are using this type of distorted thinking:
see things as either all good or totally bad?	all or nothing
always look to blame yourself or others when things don't work out well?	blaming
label people and actions, and refuse to listen to other ideas?	labeling
think you know why people act as they do without proof? base the way you act toward people on these beliefs?	mind reading
see everything as a tragedy? make small problems into big ones?	magnifying
have rules in your mind about how you and others "should" act?	shoulds
make sweeping judgments based on little proof?	overgeneralizing
feel helpless to change your life in any way?	feeling helpless

- Don't compare yourself. Your worth doesn't depend on being better than others. Your talents and abilities are your own.
- Take charge of your own life. You know your own needs and wants better than anyone else. Assert yourself. Say no to what you don't want to do. Don't assume everything has to stay the same. Focus on the choices that are open to you.
- Shift your focus. Stop looking at the problem and start looking for solutions.
- Don't try to change others. It is hard to change yourself. It is impossible to change others. Luckily, your happiness depends on you, not them.
- Listen to others. There is no single right point of view. Repeat what you hear back to the speaker to be sure you understand.
- Your life is the reward. Don't do things in hopes of being rewarded by others. Set up your life to meet some of your own needs and give yourself some pleasure.

Why Worry?

Do you worry about things you can't control? Worry and anger are harmful. They add to stress. But people often say they "can't help" worrying or being angry.

Some people worry about everything. Worrying doesn't make a problem go away. In fact, it often makes the problem worse. Worry keeps people from facing their problem and trying to solve it.

If you are worrying about a problem, ask yourself these questions:

1. What is the problem?
2. Is it really a problem? (What signs show you that it is a problem? What do you think those signs mean? Are there other ways to look at things?)
3. How important is the problem? (What would happen if you did nothing about it? What would happen if you stopped worrying?)

4. Can you do anything about the problem? (Can you change whether it will happen? Can you change its outcome?)

5. Did it already happen? (Did it affect you or someone else? Is it likely to happen again? How likely? Can you prevent it?)

6. Are you responsible for doing something about the problem? (Why? Do others agree that you are responsible? How do you know?)

You may find that there is nothing you can do to change the problem. Or that someone else is responsible for the problem. If that is the case, try to stop worrying. Stopping **negative thoughts** may help you stop worrying.

Stopping negative thoughts

Do you think negative thoughts? Think about what you tell yourself about events. When you are stuck in a traffic jam, do you say, "I'm stupid for coming this way"? Does this start you off on a string of negative thinking?

Negative thinking doesn't help. Talk back to it. Say something like "No, I'm not stupid. Everyone gets caught in traffic at one time or another. I'll plan what to do for my father's birthday while I wait."

No matter how you react, it takes the same amount of time to get out of the traffic jam. If you spend the time thinking positively, you won't wear yourself out.

When an unpleasant thought occurs, you can get rid of it. You can put it out of your mind. Try **positive thinking.**

Distract yourself by noticing everything around you. Say out loud, "Now I see the door. Now I see the pen. Now I see a tree outside the window." Keep on naming things. Name things over again if you need to. It distracts you.

Or try this. A negative thought happens. Close your eyes and focus on the thought.

Count to three. Yell the word "Stop!" as loud as you can. Repeat the process if the thought happens again. This makes it harder for you to return to your thought.

Anger

Do you get angry easily? Anger is another emotion that increases stress and gets in the way of solving problems. The amount of anger you feel depends on three things. They are:

- what happens in your body
- what you think
- what you do

You will feel anger if you think that other people are out to get you. You can make yourself more angry by planning to get even.

Your anger will increase if your body is tense and nervous. It will also increase if you yell at someone else.

If you get angry quickly, take some time to examine your **anger triggers.** For two weeks, write down all the things that make you angry. Also write down who was involved and what time of day it happened. This is your **anger log.**

At the end of two weeks, look over what you have written. Are there repeated events? Is there a time of day that is most stressful?

Once you spot some anger triggers, you can make plans to avoid or reduce them. Would a change of routine help? Do you need more sleep? Can another person handle some of the problems?

Then add some calming routines to your day. Go for a walk or practice a breathing exercise. Take time to be kind to someone else.

Think about what is important and what isn't. Be ready to laugh at yourself. Have **flexible beliefs.** Remind yourself, "Don't worry about the small stuff. And it's all small stuff." It's good advice.

You Can Change Your Beliefs

The beliefs that guide your life are another key to how much stress you feel. The following chart shows some beliefs that many people have. On the left are some **inflexible beliefs.** On the right are more flexible beliefs. Try to follow the flexible beliefs to reduce your stress.

Inflexible	Flexible
I should make sure everybody likes me.	I like approval, but trying to get it from everyone will not run my life.
People should do things right at all times.	People make mistakes. That is how we learn and improve.
The worst thing that can happen is for things in my life to go wrong.	Not getting my way is not the end of the world. I will try something else.
People can't control their thoughts and feelings.	I can change my thoughts and feelings.
People should think of every possible bad outcome before making any decision.	I don't have to expect the worst.

Inflexible	Flexible
It is better to avoid problems than face them.	When I avoid problems they often get worse. Working on a problem makes me feel better.
When things don't work out, it's usually someone else's fault.	I know what is best for me and can rely on my own judgment.
I have to worry about other people's problems.	I can help my family and friends some of the time. But they are in charge of their own lives.
There is one right answer to every problem.	There is no one right or perfect answer. I will choose a course of action and see how it works.
People should never hurt anyone else's feelings.	Even if people act with care and kindness, they are going to hurt others sometimes.

Adapted from work by Dr. Albert Ellis.
Source: American Institute for Preventive Medicine

Program Your Mind for Success

Do you always try to think of positive outcomes? Do you act out important events in your mind? Do you imagine how a job interview or first date will go?

Your mind is powerful. You can use it to shape positive attitudes and results.

You can imagine yourself getting along with your new boss. Then you may feel more confident. That may make it more likely that you will get along with him or her.

Here are some steps to follow:

1. Take a deep, relaxing breath.

2. State what the upcoming event is. (I am meeting my new boss.)

3. Create a picture in your mind of the event taking place. Make the **mental picture** as much like the actual event as you can.

4. Let yourself feel **positive emotions** like pride or joy. Smile while you are imagining it. Imagine yourself very calm and relaxed. (I feel calm and happy. I know I am going to like working for her.)

5. Practice this kind of imagining for a few minutes in the morning and at night.

Knowing When You Need Help

You can do a lot on your own to handle stress. But sometimes, stress may get too bad for you to handle by yourself. That's when you need professional help. You can get help from counseling or a self-help group. Your doctor can help you find something right for you.

The first step is knowing that you need help. Here are some signs to look for:

- You feel like you have lost control of your life.
- You have problems dealing with people.
- You feel hopeless, confused, or frustrated.
- You don't enjoy anything anymore.

- You feel great, then you feel awful (or the other way around).
- You feel depressed for weeks or months.
- You do things to hurt yourself or others.
- You have problems with sex.
- You have trouble sleeping for weeks or months.
- You feel afraid for no reason.
- You think about killing yourself.
- You think about being sick all the time.
- You drink a lot of alcohol or take drugs.

To find out more

- Ask your doctor for suggestions.
- Look in your local paper for support groups.
- Ask your employer if your company provides any services to help employees cope with stress.
- Look in the phone book under Social Services, Mental Health Services, or Stress Management Programs.

Chapter 10

Life Stories, Continued

Remember the life stories at the start of this book? Using some of the methods in this book, those people were able to reduce their stress and improve their lives. Here's how.

Ann

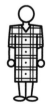 Ann got more and more worried about her short temper. She began to feel that her children were afraid of her. And her work suffered because she had so much on her mind.

One day, Ann saw an ad for a support group for divorced parents. The ad said that the members shared ideas and feelings about family, work, and stress. Ann felt like she needed someone to talk to who understood her life. Nobody at work seemed to have the same problems. She called the number and went to the next meeting.

She didn't say much that first night. Just listening to the others helped. At the next meeting, Ann talked about her divorce and her kids. She shared her feelings with the group.

After a while, Ann started calling her friends again. Before work, she now exercises for about 20 minutes. She feels less tense the rest of the day and sleeps better at night.

One of the things the support group talked about was listening. Ann learned that listening to her kids is as important as talking to them. Now, she works hard to really hear what her kids are telling her. She and her kids seem to get along much better.

Robert

 Robert missed work twice because of a hangover from drinking. He was worried he'd lose his job. A co-worker asked him why he looked so stressed.

The co-worker understood many of Robert's problems. She had a high stress level, too. They talked about managing stress. They both had some ideas. First, Robert knew he had to cut down on his drinking.

Robert needed to take care of himself better. That included making other people understand his needs. Now, he tries to be more honest with his boss. It turns out that the boss likes many of Robert's ideas about how to do the job.

The softball team at work invited Robert to join. Now that he gets some exercise, he's feeling better. He's also starting to feel that he belongs at work.

Robert is making changes in his daily life one at a time. He's eating regular meals and trying to follow guidelines for healthy eating. He's even starting to stand up to his father. He listens more carefully to his father and responds, instead of clamming up.

Robert's stress level is lower than before. He still has problems to deal with, but he's coping better with his daily life.

Jon

 Jon didn't take his sister's advice about seeing a doctor right away. He kept on working long hours, smoking too much, and leaving the apartment a mess. His work suffered, and his boss

noticed it. When his boss talked to him about it, Jon knew something had to change.

Jon made an appointment with his doctor. He told him about the stress in his life and his problems. The doctor suggested a few things.

The doctor showed Jon how to build exercise into his daily life. Now, Jon gets off the bus a few blocks from work and walks the rest of the way. He uses stairs whenever he can, instead of elevators. He never uses the remote control for the TV.

The biggest change Jon made was in his smoking. He still smokes, but is trying to quit. He doesn't light up first thing in the morning. Instead, he does deep breathing and stretching when he wakes up. He notices how much better he feels afterward.

Jon has more energy. He's started to care more about his life again. He eats regular meals and avoids junk food. Jon keeps the apartment in better shape and takes pride in it.

Glossary

absolutes: definite things that don't allow any discussion or change

additives: chemicals added to food to keep it fresh, to give flavor or color, or to add nutrients

aerobic exercise: exercise that makes the heart pump faster and gets more air into the lungs

anger log: a record of when you are angry, what made you angry, and what you did

anger triggers: things that always make you angry

anxiety: a feeling of being very upset or nervous

blood pressure: how fast blood pumps around the body

burnout: having very little energy or interest in life. Burnout often comes after a high-stress period.

caffeine: a chemical substance found mostly in coffee, tea, and chocolate. It is a stimulant that people can get addicted to.

cholesterol: a substance in animal fat that can build up inside the body and cause heart disease

coping: finding ways to keep going

distorted thinking: looking at only one side of an issue and ignoring the others

fiber: a substance that helps the body get rid of waste and keeps the digestive system strong

flexible beliefs: beliefs that you can change

food log: a record of when you eat, what you eat, how much you eat, and why you eat

hyperactive: too much energy or jumpiness

"I-messages": saying things that focus on you, the speaker

inflexible beliefs: beliefs that you won't change

junk food: foods that are high in empty calories but low in nutrients. Most junk foods contain a lot of fat, sugar, or sodium.

long-term goal: a goal likely to have a lasting effect on your life. It may take some time to fulfill.

manage stress: keep your stress under control

master calendar: a large, central calendar

mental picture: a picture in your mind

negative thoughts: thinking about the bad things that have happened or might happen

nutrients: the useful materials the body gets from food

positive emotions: feelings that make you feel happy or good about yourself

positive thinking: thinking about the good things that have happened or might happen

priorities: what is most important to you

protein: a nutrient that helps the body make new cells and repair itself

shallow (breathing): when you don't breathe deeply

short-term goals: goals likely to help you get through your daily life and that you can fulfill quite quickly

stress: how your mind and body react to what happens in your life

stress level: how much stress you have

stress notebook: a notebook in which you write anything that can help you manage your stress

stressors: things that cause you stress

thinking patterns: the way you usually think

time log: a record of how you spend your time and how long each task takes

"Type A" person: a person who has a high level of stress because they think they have to be perfect. They try to do more than they can, don't trust others, and get angry a lot.

"Type B" behavior: low-key behavior that is calm and shows that someone is taking life at a steady pace

5/10